HEAD INJURY -

A FAMILY NIGHTMARE

BY

ESTELLE FLYNN

authorHOUSE®

AuthorHouse™
1663 Liberty Drive
Bloomington, IN 47403
www.authorhouse.com
Phone: 1-800-839-8640

First published by AuthorHouse 05/03/2011

ISBN: 978-1-4567-5179-1 (e)
ISBN: 978-1-4567-5180-7 (sc)

Library of Congress Control Number: 2011903742

Printed in the United States of America

Any people depicted in stock imagery provided by Thinkstock are models,
and such images are being used for illustrative purposes only.
Certain stock imagery © Thinkstock.
Some names have been changed for privacy reasons.
This book is printed on acid-free paper.

TABLE OF CONTENTS

Why This Book Was Written 1

That Awful Day 3

The Diagnosis 6

Care At Lower Bucks Hospital 8

The Operation 10

Hospital Rehabilitation 11

At Home Rehabilitation 15

Teaching Tools 16

Meet The Family 18

And Then There Were None 25

Our Support 26

Back To School 27

"Head On" 29

Moving On 31

On His Own 33

My Own Near Breakdown 35

Back To My Roots 37

The Marriage Not Made In Heaven 38

A Visit To The Enchanted Land *41*

The Divorce *43*

The Good Samaritan *44*

Time To Call In The Law *46*

On Being Vulnerable *47*

Losing It All *48*

Bringing Danny Home *50*

Seeking Help *51*

The Reality *55*

My Last Encounter *57*

Epilogue *60*

WHY THIS BOOK WAS WRITTEN

For thirty-four years I have searched book stores and libraries for information on head injury, and how other families were coping with it. The most I came up with were books containing medical terms that I, as a lay person, could not understand. Therefore I decided to write my own story about our family and what we've endured for the past thirty-four years. My husband and I and our other three children suffered at different times and in different ways coping with Danny's many injuries, but in particular his head injury. We had some good times as well as bad, but things will never be the same. All of our lives were changed in one day. Now our lives are relatively normal, at least to the outside world. Thanks to the many prayers, the help and support of our many friends, we now find few obstacles that we cannot overcome; we've learned to cope, at least to some extent.

I especially want people who have a head injured love one to understand that there are things they should be aware of and that they should be on guard against people who might take advantage of someone with a disability. A head injury is more difficult to spot because there are no visible infirmities such as wheelchairs, walkers, canes or bandages. Every head injured person is different, most often it is only through holding a conversation with that person that you become aware that the head injured person is different, and sadly, sometimes people even think the person is mentally ill or under the influence of drugs or alcohol.

Head injury is now more prevalent than it was thirty-four years ago due to accidents, sports injuries, many more motorcycles on the roads, and the great number of men and women returning from wars with TBI (traumatic brain injury). Granted the treatment they receive is far more advanced than it was thirty-four years ago, but it is still just as traumatic when it happens as it was in 1977. Trust me, we've been there and been through it all. So please, stay alert and informed because you never know when your family could be affected by TBI.

THAT AWFUL DAY

The accident happened on May 8, 1977, Mother's Day. I had made a turkey dinner and we were waiting for Danny and his friend, Nancy, to come home from church. They didn't want to stay for dinner because they were in a hurry. They were to meet their friends at the school lot for a baseball game and were already late. Danny, at that time, was working at a local seafood restaurant and was to start at 5:00 PM. He said that since Mother's Day was always one of their busiest days of the year, he wanted to go in an hour early to give the other workers a hand. But he also wanted to play a little baseball before he had to leave.

One of his young friends had just purchased a motorcycle that week and had it at the field. He knew everyone would want to see it and maybe even take it for a ride. Danny never had any desire to own a motorcycle, he loved his fancy blue Road Runner car.

Nancy wanted Danny to take her for a ride around the block before he had to leave for work. I don't suppose any eighteen year old young man wants to admit he doesn't know much about driving a motorcycle, so they put on their helmets, drove one half block, hit the gravel on the road at the intersection, and landed under a truck that was parked on the corner.

About 3:30 PM several of Danny's friends came running in our door to tell us that Danny and Nancy had a bad accident and we should hurry to the emergency room at Lower Bucks Hospital where the ambulance had taken Danny and Nancy. The sight of his injuries, especially his face with his left eye bulging and black and blood everywhere, overwhelmed us. Nancy had been transferred to another hospital where, two weeks later, she succumbed to her injuries. Many of Danny's friends who were at the ball field also came to the hospital. They told us that George, one of the friends, had given Danny CPR until the ambulance arrived. That probably saved his life. They also brought the helmets they were wearing at the time of the accident. They were pretty banged up, but upon examining them I suspect that the helmets were not buckled. This was never proven, probably couldn't be, but it remains a thought in my mind.

The neurosurgeon on duty that day was a doctor from another country who we could not understand. This made us even more confused and anxious. Several nurses at the hospital suggested we contact another neurosurgeon affiliated with the hospital. We could get a second opinion and perhaps be more comfortable with a doctor we could understand and get answers to our many questions. We contacted the late Dr. William Sagan and requested that he be assigned as Danny's neurosurgeon.

About three weeks later, when he felt Danny was stabilized enough to be moved, Dr. Sagan arranged to have a CAT scan done at Temple University Hospital in Philadelphia. The test had to be done there because they didn't have the equipment necessary for this test at our local hospital. The CAT scan was a new technology at that time, and in addition to not being available at any of the local hospitals, it was still considered experimental, and therefore, was not covered by our health insurance.

THE DIAGNOSIS

In addition to his head injury Danny suffered many other cuts and bruises and a broken collar bone which was reset but never healed properly, so today it is crooked. At this point Danny was also blind. We called in our family eye specialist who came to the hospital to examine Danny's eyes. He said he had treated many cases like this when he was in the Air Force in World War II. He explained to us that first Danny would have double vision, but in time his eyesight should return. And that is exactly the way it happened, though it took many, many months. We were so grateful for this!

On June 4, 1977 about 9:00 AM we left Lower Bucks Hospital in the ambulance, heading for Temple Hospital for the CAT scan. I rode in the back with Danny, holding his hands. He was still blind and semi-conscious. At the hospital he was placed on a gurney in the hallway where we waited almost ten hours for the Scan to be taken. I stood next to Danny, holding his hands and talking to him, so that he knew I was there. I'm sure he was scared because he didn't know what was happening. Several times some very kind nurses from Temple came by and offered to stay with him while I went to the restroom or to get a drink. They knew we had been there a very long time. Finally he was wheeled into the Scan room, but they had to come out and get me, put me in a rubber suit and have me hold his hands because he was shaking so badly. Subconsciously, I'm sure he was very frightened, however he could not communicate to us and we didn't know if he understood what we were telling him.

We arrived back at Lower Bucks Hospital about 10:00 PM, where my husband had been waiting nervously all day for our return. We came home exhausted, still not knowing the results of the test Danny had taken.

The CAT scan showed that Danny had Hydrocephalus, water on the brain, causing the brain to shrink. Dr. Sagan explained to us how he would implant a shunt into Danny's head. The shunt would run from his brain to his jugular vein and thus return the water to his body, where it would be harmless. This would allow room for the brain to enlarge to its normal size and eventually heal, at least to some point. His prognosis was not encouraging. My husband and I were told that any recovery would take a long time, and the outcome questionable.

CARE AT LOWER BUCKS HOSPITAL

Danny stayed at Lower Bucks Hospital about two more weeks while his physical injuries were being taken care of and he was having physical, speech, and occupational therapies.

The nurses caring for him were wonderful! Because Danny still could not get out of bed they bathed him in the bed. At the time Danny had long, straight hair, the 70's style. Two nurses would lay him sideways over the bed, so his head was hanging down. They put a bucket underneath his head and proceeded to shampoo his hair. I was amazed watching them, and they would be joking with him all the while. Even though he wasn't fully conscious I know he enjoyed this. Whenever his temperature went too high they would put an ice mattress under him to bring it down. It always worked.

He never had visitors other than family members in the hospital. That was my doing. I didn't want his friends to see him in his present condition. And knowing nothing about coma, I was sure he would just wake up one day (I guess that I watched too many medical shows on TV!) and he would recognize everyone, and immediately speak in full sentences, with all his memories and education intact. I feared that one of his friends would come to visit him and talk about the accident, especially about Nancy. I knew that if he learned about Nancy's death he would be devastated.

Then there was the day of the fire at the hospital. The fire alarm went off, the nurses rushed to shut all the doors of the patient rooms and I could smell the smoke. Danny was on the fourth floor in the front of the hospital, so I could look out the windows and see the firemen and trucks. I panicked! The fire was on the fourth floor, just down the hall. Luckily he had a great roommate, an older man named Marty, who promised me that if the fire reached us, he and I could lift Danny out of the bed and put him on the ledge that was just outside their room. I knew that this was impossible, but Marty kept convincing me it could be done. Although we were of different faiths he suggested we pray together, which we did. Finally the fire was put out and we were all safe. But without Marty I don't know what I would have done. We found out later that the fire was started by a man who was smoking in his bed.

THE OPERATION

Ten days after the CAT scan, on June 14, 1977, Danny had half his head shaved and the shunt was implanted. That evening when Dr. Sagan came in to check on him, he took his hand and twisted Danny's head, and Danny cried "Ouch!" the first word we heard him utter in six weeks. We were ecstatic to hear him speak! But Dr. Sagan told us not to be too optimistic, for Danny still had a long way to go, and it was possible that if the shunt didn't work we'd have to place him in a nursing home for the extensive twenty-four hour a day care he would need due to his head injury. He didn't wake up and start speaking, but he did begin to make small, gradual improvements after the shunt was implanted.

HOSPITAL REHABILITATION

After about another month at Lower Bucks Hospital Danny was transferred to Moss Rehabilitation Hospital in Philadelphia. He hated it there because the rehabilitation was intense; he still didn't have his eyesight back, and was very angry and agitated. We were called three times from the hospital to come and get him because they couldn't handle him. By this time he was experiencing double vision. At that time most rehabilitation hospitals did not have special units for head injured victims, but we were advised that this was the best place for him to be. Rehabilitation hospitals were geared toward physical rehabilitation only. The staff at Moss did get Danny to stand and even take a few hesitant steps with help, but they were not able to address his brain injury. I believe we were discovering the true effects of head injury at this time.

Between my husband and I, and my two sisters Anne and Carly, we took turns staying with Danny every day until it was his bedtime. The worst part was that every night they would tie him into bed on his back to make sure he didn't try and get out of bed. I wanted to make sure they gave him medication to make him sleep. I found out that they gave him Ambien every night. Some times I wonder how I ever drove home from Philadelphia without having an accident, because I would cry all the way home. Even now, thirty-four years later, he cannot sleep unless his light or his television is on.

I wasn't too good at sleeping either. I had too much to worry about. Danny had lawsuits pending from everyone. We had to hire lawyers because there was no way we could pay the enormous amount of debt that Danny was facing. We had to go before our District Judge to tell him that it could be years until Danny was rehabilitated enough to get a job and pay the fine he received from him (which in the end we paid).

One Sunday the Rehabilitation Hospital let us bring Danny home for the day for his brother Michael's third birthday. Danny wasn't too aware of what was going on, but he knew he was home. We saw our neighbors looking out their windows to gawk at him because he was so thin and he could walk only with help. They weren't being nosy, but truly concerned because they knew how much he had gone through. We had a nice day, Danny was happy to be home. He recognized Michael, but we weren't sure if he recognized the rest of us, either family or neighbors because he called us all by different names, but names familiar to him. He even got his dad and I mixed up!

The sad part came when he had to go back to Moss, he didn't understand why he had to leave home. It took my husband and two brothers-in-law to get him in the car, it was another heart break. We all had tears running down our faces as the car pulled away.

The next week they let him come home and stay overnight. Since he was still very confused, I was afraid he would think he was still at the hospital and try to leave. So when he fell asleep in his own bed I tied a rope around his ankle and extended it to my wrist (I slept on the couch), and then to the back door. That way, if he got up during the night the rope would wake me up. Not that I slept much that night anyway. Thankfully he didn't get up. I think he was happy being in his own bed. That's when my husband and I decided it was time to bring him home, we would manage him ourselves.

The first thing we did on the way home from the hospital was to stop at Dr. Sagan's office (our neurosurgeon). Dr.

Sagan told us to take Danny off the Ambien medication that he had been on at Moss. He examined his shunt and said it was working fine. He said there was something like a little wheel at the base of the shunt, and he could feel it, although we never could. He said if there was ever a change in Danny, we would notice it, and should call him immediately. Luckily we've never had to do this, and the shunt has been in place thirty-four years. Dr. Sagan also said that once Danny regained his eyesight, his Dad should take him to an empty parking lot and let him drive his car. It was quite a while before we were ready to begin letting Danny get behind the wheel of a car. The first time they tried his Dad said it was as if Danny never stopped driving. They practiced driving until his Dad felt he could go somewhere familiar and then find his way home without Dad's prompting. They did this many times, but Danny always knew where he was going and how to get home. Dan frequently drove a couple of blocks to visit his cousins who live in the same neighborhood as we do. It was as if the part of his memory that controls driving and directions had not been affected at all.

AT HOME REHABILITATION

When we got home we began our own rehabilitation. We had to teach Danny how to feed himself, how to walk, how to talk, how to brush his teeth, how to use the bathroom facilities, basically everything a child has to be taught from birth. Every night his Dad would give him a shower, we were so afraid that he might slip and fall. The simplest daily activities took much longer than anticipated. Walking from one room to the next was an effort due to his impaired eyesight and his overall weakness. After so much time in the hospital Danny had lost a lot of weight and muscle mass. We also spent time looking through photo albums trying to help Danny remember names and faces of family members, most of whom he had known his whole life, but could not recall.

TEACHING TOOLS

Before Danny's accident I used to teach Remedial Reading to students in grades three to eight at St. Joseph the Worker School in Fallsington. I started to use some of the things that I used with those children with Danny. I made up index cards and put the letters of the alphabet on each side, one side for capital letters and the other side for lower case letters. Once he got them down I made up cards with words printed on them. I started with simple words like "cat" and "boy", then moved on to harder words like "picture" and "something". Then we went to the really big words like "automobile" and "transportation". From using words, we graduated to making sentences. I would scramble the word cards out on the table and have him pick words that made sentences. It was one of our "fun games". Another game we played was "Bingo". I took 9 x 12" papers and made nine squares on each paper. The X in the middle square was "free". The other eight boxes had words in them. I would give him a word. If he had it on his paper he could cover it with a red plastic marker. If he got three squares in a road, up, down or diagonally he would yell "Bingo"!

Although Danny was originally awarded Social Security Disability Insurance (SSDI), the decision was reversed, and the money had to be paid back. I searched agency after agency to no avail. It was determined that as long as Danny was capable of menial labor, such as washing dishes, he would not qualify for SSDI. We tried to find him a job that would be repetitious, like an assembly line in a factory. But as soon as we mentioned that he was head injured he was turned down. Every place Danny applied for work was able to find a "more qualified" candidate for the job. As I said, at that time people didn't understand head injury and were afraid of it. Our government agencies were no help at all; they passed the buck from one agency to another.

MEET THE FAMILY

Let me introduce our family. My name is Estelle and I am Danny's mother. I enjoy reading, swimming, writing, playing the piano, organ and harp and am an organist at St. Ann Church in Bristol, Pa. I have always been a volunteer in both church and community organizations. i.e. Girl Scout Leader, Board of Elections, Falls Township Cultural Arts Commission, Meals on Wheels driver, Director of two Children's Choirs, served seven years on the Board of Directors of the Pennsylvania Head Injury Foundation, and founder of "Head On", a support group for Head Injured individuals.

Danny's father is Francis. He is retired from A.T.&T., and likes reading, gardening, and sudoku and crossword puzzles. He served as a member of our church Financial Committee, was Chairman of the church Social Organization and was Treasurer of the Catholic Youth Organization for several years. His help and support enabled me to finally write this book.

Danny is our oldest child. He was eighteen at the time of his accident. He attended St. Joseph the Worker Elementary School in Fallsington, Pa. graduated from Bishop Egan High School in 1976 and was working at a popular Seafood Restaurant in Langhorne, Pa.

Danny was always a hard worker, always wanted to earn money to put in his bank account, with the dream of someday owning his own car. When he was twelve he became a paper delivery boy for the Bucks County Courier Times, and by the time he was sixteen and in high school he had two jobs. He worked every day after school at Bakers Shoe Store in the Oxford Valley Mall, and on week-ends he worked at Seafood Shanty in Langhorne. We told all our children that if they wanted to drive and own a car they had to work in order to maintain the car, pay their own car insurance and gas, upkeep, and so forth. They also had to maintain good grades in school. Danny met the requirements.

Danny always loved fishing and for the past five years has been a member of our local fishing club at Levittown Lake. He is also a member of the local V.F.W. (his dad is a Korean War veteran), where he likes to play darts and have a couple of beers! For the past twenty-seven years he has been a volunteer, twice a week, at our church Bingo. For the same number of years he has also been a volunteer usher at the Noon Mass on Sunday at our church.

Our daughter, Erin, was seventeen at the time of the accident and was about to graduate from Bishop Conwell High School in Levittown. Because we were spending most of our time at the hospital with Danny, Erin took a lot of responsibility for her baby brother that summer, and understood why there would be no graduation celebrations for her. She was afraid we would miss her graduation, but was relieved when she saw her Dad and I enter the school just in time for the ceremonies to begin. We were happy, surprised, and proud when it was announced that she was awarded a grant to Marywood College in Scranton, Pa. Erin spent two years at Marywood before transferring to Allentown College in Center Valley, Pa. (now called De Sales University). After graduation from college she went on to earn her MBA, with a specialization in Human Resources, and was nationally certified as a Senior Professional in Human Resources. She went on to have a successful twenty-five year career.

In October, 1986 Erin married Richard Paglione and in May, 1988 presented us with our first grandchild,

Laura Ann, our darling, sweet girl. Laura recently graduated from De Sales University where she majored in English in the hopes of becoming an editor or a writer.

Danny's accident was a little harder on our third child, Jimmy. He was only twelve years old at the time, old enough to know the seriousness of it, but not old enough to know what to do to help. He, too, attended St. Joseph the Worker Elementary School and graduated from Bishop Egan High School in 1982. Although he was very smart he didn't want to go to college. Instead he went to Pennco Technical School in Bristol, Pa. where he graduated in the top ten in his class and was offered a job immediately with a major communications corporation. When things slowed down there he took a job with a pipeline company in Allentown, Pa. where he still works as an I.T. Professional. While still working he completed seven years of night school at DeSales University to get his degree in Computer Science and graduated Cum Laude.

In November, 1987 Jimmy married Noreen Polcha and they are the parents of two sons. Their son, Andrew, is now 17 years old, very intelligent, and plays the piano beautifully by note and by ear. He is an exceptionally good artist, and draws and writes cartoons for his school newspaper. He hopes to become a film animator and to that end he and his parent are looking into colleges that offer the courses he will need. Their younger son, Ryan, who is now 14, plays drums in his school band, likes skateboarding, art, and plays on an Ice Hockey team, which his dad coaches. Together the family likes to ski, go out on their sailboat, travel (especially out West), and play with Ceili, their dog.

Our youngest son, Michael, was the easiest to acclimate to Danny's change of personality. He was only two when the accident happened, so he doesn't know what Danny was like pre-accident. When Danny was in the hospital they let us bring baby Michael in to sit on Danny's lap. Even though Danny was still in a semi-conscious state and had no sight, he recognized Michael and would grin from ear to ear when the baby sat with him. To this day, Danny always says it was Michael who "woke him up" from his coma.

Michael graduated from Bishop Egan High School in 1992 and then graduated from Bucks County Community College where he received certification in bio-technology. He then worked at a chemical lab in Bristol, Pa., where he earned a patent for lightweight structure finish. He continues to work as a lab research technician.

In October, 2000 he married Kellie Steen and in November 2003 they had their first child, Sean Michael, our little angel! Sean was born four months premature weighing in at 15.4 ounces. He spent four months in the neo-natal intensive care unit at the University of Pennsylvania Hospital. We never thought he would survive. His skin was so transparent you could see every vein in his body, many are still visible now at seven years of age. But the family and his doctors never gave up on him; the doctors said he was a fighter, and they were right! The wonderful doctors and nurses who cared for him at the Hospital of the University of Pennsylvania were magnificent. He was sent home after four months, weighing four pounds. His mom had a difficult delivery by caesarean section but thankfully recovered within a matter of weeks.

Sean is now in first grade and is doing very well. He loves school and gets along great with both his classmates and his teachers. He has speech and occupational therapy and we were told by the doctors it may take him a few years to catch up to his classmates, but he's progressing very well. He's a very happy child, and when he enters our front door he brings a ray of sunshine with him!

It is happily ironic that it is Michael's son who is the beneficiary of substantial medical breakthroughs and therapies that are available today, which allow him to progress and thrive along with his classmates. A baby born under one pound would have had no chance of survival at the time of Danny's accident in 1977. Danny believes it was Michael who got him through the coma when medical science could not and it was medical science that returned the favor by allowing Michael to have his own son.

AND THEN THERE WERE NONE

After we brought Danny home to stay, his friends rarely came by to see him, and that hurt. It took me about twelve years to get over my anger at them. But I finally realized that Danny was not the same person they knew before his accident. If they took him out, he acted inappropriately and embarrassed them. They couldn't accept his change in personality, and looking back now I can't blame them. They were not responsible for his social life. He was our responsibility only. They went on with their lives, married, and had children, while Danny was at a standstill socially. His Dad was a volunteer at our church Bingo twice a week and two Fridays a month. He got Danny to volunteer also, and he loved it. It was a chance to meet and talk to many people and also gave him a sense of responsibility. And the people responded to his cheerfulness. It's been thirty years now, and although his father retired, Danny still goes faithfully. Likewise, about the same time he volunteered to serve as an usher at our Sunday Noon Mass, and still commits to that every week.

OUR SUPPORT

During all this time we were lucky to receive loving support from our family and friends. Many prayers were said by individuals and prayer groups for Danny. And my two sisters, Carly and Anne, were our crutches. They saw to the care of our other children, handled the many phone calls and provided both food and comfort. They lifted many a burden off our shoulders by always being available. We brought both a radio and tape player into the hospital to put by Danny's bed so he could listen to what we called "The crazy music of the 70's". Carly would tell him that when he came home from the hospital he would have to sit with her every Saturday night to listen to Lawrence Welk, just to get even. This usually caused him to give her half a smile, so we knew he understood her. And baby Michael would make tapes saying "Danny, hurry and get home, I'm washing your car and making it nice and clean for you.", and other things a three year old would say. Danny understood this too and would smile when he heard Michael's voice.

BACK TO SCHOOL

Once Danny was able to resume driving, we sent him to Bucks County Community College for remedial reading and math. Then we sent him to a Heating and Air-Conditioning School in Philadelphia, but he couldn't grasp that. Meanwhile, a relative of ours got Danny a job in a sheet metal plant, where Danny worked for twenty-one years. He worked twelve hours a day, Monday to Friday and six hours on Saturday. He never took a vacation. He stayed instead to clean out the large vats that had to be done once a year. Danny was always a good worker, he always wanted money in his bank. When he was fourteen years old he got a job delivering the Bucks County Courier Times. By the time he was sixteen and in high school, he had two jobs. Every day after school he worked at Baker's Shoe Store in the Oxford Valley Mall, and on the week-ends he worked at Seafood Shanty, a restaurant in Langhorne, Pa. His objective was to get a car. His father and I told him if he wanted a car he had to be able to maintain it, pay his own insurance and drive responsibly. And that is how he came to buy and to love his Road Runner, the car he had the day of his motorcycle accident.

"HEAD ON"

Back in 1977 when we made our first post-operative visit to his neurosurgeon we were perplexed, now what we do? He said to go home, forget that Danny has a shunt in his head, and lead as normal life as we could. That wasn't the answer I wanted to hear. I said I was sure we were not the only family suffering through a crisis like this. He didn't have an answer. So I contacted Danny's Speech Therapist and asked her if she knew and families in situations like ours. She put me in touch with three other families and we had our first "Head On" meeting in our home. This was to be a support group for head injured victims and their families. By sharing our stories we hoped to pass along information to others, and to get the help of people in the medical profession for advice. I was told that this was the first support group of its kind in Pennsylvania, and possibly in the nation. I then received permission from a local hospital to place notices in their emergency room, and to hold our monthly meetings in their hospital. We met on the first Thursday of every month. The hospital was kind enough to provide coffee and tea. On the way to the meeting I would stop at a local donut shop and they would give me all the doughnuts they had left over from that day. I invited doctors, lawyers, psychologists, school administrators, police department representatives, anyone interested in learning about this devastating illness, and we never had a lack of guests, as we educated each other. One incident in particular comes to mind. Reading the newspaper one morning I saw that one of our members, whose mother was dead and father was distant, was arrested the night before while walking along a main road and charged with being drunk. They didn't understand that he was head injured, was not able to walk normal, and had no one looking out for him. This was brought up at our next meeting, at which two policemen showed up, and we asked them to share this with all other police officers.

We were blessed with a lot of help and advice from Dr. Dan Keating, who at the time was a psychologist at Moss Rehab. He attended many of our "Head On" meetings here in Bucks County, even though he lived quite a distance away from us. He even came to see Danny at a time when we most needed him, because Danny was completely out of control. Dr. Keating made himself available to our entire "Head On" group and was a great supporter of our work.

MOVING ON

Within six months I was asked by Moss Rehabilitation Hospital to help them set up a "Pennsylvania Head Injury Foundation", which I did. I visited hospitals around the state advising them how to start a support group in their communities. I served on the Board of Directors for seven years, but came to realize that while I was trying to help others, I could get no help for my own son, particularly when it came time to finding employment. He had short-term memory problems, but I knew he could work if given a job that was repetitive. And that was proven when he was hired by the manufacturing company that gave him the chance he needed. While Danny was still at Moss the psychiatrist explained that his mind was like a puzzle where the pieces had to be put back together. He felt this condition would improve in time, but he could not promise this because there was not enough research done on head injury yet. Danny remembered some things like our summer vacations at Lake Cadjaw in the Pocono Mountains, where he liked to swim, boat, and fish. But he couldn't remember graduating from High School, although he did remember the Senior Class trip he took to Mexico.

We were fortunate that both Erin and Jimmy seemed to understand what we were dealing with and they never complained. Beginning in September after Danny's accident Erin was away at college and was only home a few times each year. She was content staying at school however, because besides her school work, she was very involved in the theater program and spent a lot of time working on costumes, sets, and lighting for the Theater and Music departments. She was also president of a community service organization on campus, and spent time organizing and working on various events.

Jimmy, on the other hand, was home and he took the brunt of Danny's frustrations, to the point where Danny would try to physically attack him. Jimmy would not retaliate because he knew that Danny was hurting in his own way. When Jimmy would ignore him, Danny took out his anger on the walls in the house, resulting in some holes in the walls. That was a very sad time for Dad and I because we remembered how much he loved Jimmy when he was born and how he liked to play with him. But we think that issue has been solved, and we are thankful that period in our lives is over.

ON HIS OWN

Once Danny was able to find steady employment he moved out of our house and into an apartment in a very nice complex near our home. We thought the independence was something he could handle and it was what he wanted to do.

One Saturday morning I woke up early and had a terrible feeling that something was wrong at Danny's. My husband had gone to work and I assumed Danny did too. But my intuition made me get right up, get dressed and rush to his apartment. Danny's car was not there and the door was locked. I had a feeling someone was in there and I banged on the door for several minutes. I spotted one of the maintenance men who worked at the complex and explained my fears to him and asked if he could let me in the apartment. He agreed to do that. On the way to the apartment I saw a young, scruffy looking man carrying bags of things, leaving the complex but looking back at us very suspiciously. The maintenance man unlocked the door for me and then left. Danny's apartment was *on the second floor. I bravely (and foolishly) walked up the stairs and found two young girls, one in the bed and the other on the couch, both obviously drunk or doped. I guess I screamed like a banshee to get them to leave. They, in turn, screamed at me and told me to get out, because they were friends of the guy who lived there and he told them they could stay until he came home from work. I finally got them to leave and they took the same path that the man who I spoke about took. I don't know where I got the courage to do such a bold and stupid thing. My family was very upset when they found out what I did, because they said these girls could have had a gun or a knife in their possession, and could have attacked me. But I was in such a rage I wasn't even thinking about the consequences of my actions. I just think God sent my angels to protect me.*

One thing I was sure of, however, was that we had to get Danny out of there; it wasn't safe for him to be on his own. He probably met these people the night before at a bar, and in his vulnerability, agreed to let them stay at his apartment that night. His apartment was leased for one year and he was only in it a month or so. In order for him to get out of his lease, his Dad and I had to pay a huge amount of money to the complex.

MY OWN NEAR BREAKDOWN

The stress of all that was happening was finally getting to me. It got to the point that I didn't think I could handle anything, the injury, my family, my church, my involvement with anyone. I just wanted to run away. One morning my sister Carly stopped by and I was in my bedroom getting a box down off the shelf. She asked me what I was doing. I said I was running away. She asked where I was going. I said I didn't know, I just knew I had to get away. I was packing clothes, have no idea what; I had no money on me to speak of, I just didn't know what I was doing, but I had to escape. She took me in her car right to the local Mental Health Center. Up to this time I hadn't sought out any help for myself because I didn't feel I needed it. Since my husband was still working I felt I had to handle all of Danny's daytime appointments, which were almost daily. Dad helped me as much as he could, and certainly worked with Danny at night, but there were so many other things regarding Erin, Jimmy and Michael that needed our attention. Everything became too much.

At the mental health center I was assigned a psychologist to work with me. I saw her once a week for about two years. I also got Danny help from there, since we could not afford a personal psychologist. He still goes there, about once every other month. I stopped going because I didn't feel the weekly talks were helping me. As I was sitting there I kept thinking about something else I should be doing, somewhere else where I should be. My mind was always racing ahead to do more. My family doctor finally convinced me to see a personal psychologist. We (Danny, Dad and I) saw this doctor about thirty times over several years and to this day there are still times when I must see him. Danny continues to go to the Mental Health Clinic.

BACK TO MY ROOTS

I was born and raised in Scranton, PA, the youngest of thirteen children. We always lived in the same house. It was a happy home, a home filled with music and love. After the deaths of my father and mother, my brother John remained in the house. It was a big house and he maintained it until his death in June 2003. It was then willed to my sisters Carly, Anne and I, with an account he kept separately to keep the house maintained, which we have to this day. This proved to be a haven for me, when things seemed too much for me I was able to go to my other home for two or three days, or on week-ends while Dad was home. (I might add Dad was never the worrier that I was, he had a calm disposition and always looked on the bright side of things, where I was completely opposite.) And since our Scranton home was just a half block away from the church we always attended growing up, I was free to spend a lot of time there, praying, meditating, walking the grounds around the stations of the cross. It was a source of peace for me.

THE MARRIAGE NOT MADE IN HEAVEN

Danny still lacked the thing he wanted most, companionship. It happened one night when he met a girl in a bar named Marcy, who became his constant companion. Although my husband and I were a little skeptical, we accepted her and welcomed her to our family functions. They were married in June, 1988 and almost immediately our suspicions were confirmed. She was estranged from her parents, so of course we paid for her bridal shower and also their large wedding. They bought a mobile home and Marcy was settled in, she won the prize she was seeking. Her idea of being a wife was to stay in bed all day, while Danny was at work, and stay up all night watching television. She refused to work, even when Erin got her a job at her company. On several occasions we found out that when Marcy said she had a job, she did not. She told Danny that she left for work after he did, and arrived home before him. Danny was working so many hours that he believed her. In reality, she was not leaving the house at all. Danny was handing over his paycheck to her every Friday, but *would go to work every morning with no lunch, (unless he found something, usually left over from us) and was able to make his own lunch. After working twelve hours every day at the machine shop he would come home to no dinner. Then he would come to us to get something to eat. Where was all the money going? They had nothing to show for it. All of their furniture was given to them, including Danny's bedroom set we bought him, and she sold most of it. All of the money they received for their wedding, plus all of the $100.00 savings bonds we bought them over the years were cashed in without Danny's knowledge.*

One day Marcy's parents came to our home to talk to us. They told us that she had filed for bankruptcy before, while she was still single. They realized that Marcy and Danny were deep in debt, and that Marcy was considering filing for bankruptcy again. I think they expected us to give them the money to bail Marcy and Danny out. Even with Marcy not working, they should not have been living above their means. We had no way to account for all the money that had gone missing. Now my husband and I suspected there were drugs involved, but we couldn't prove it. We saw Danny every day, and we noticed his anger about not having any food in his house, and about bills that were not being paid. If the telephone rang at night and Danny answered it, Marcy told him to tell the person calling that she had just mailed a check. All things considered, his home life and his bank account dwindling, it's no wonder he came here every night like a bomb ready to explode! I got to the point where I hated to see his car pull up at 6:00 PM. We found out much later that in addition to all of the bills that had gone into collection, Marcy had been collecting Unemployment checks that Danny was not aware of. When Marcy filed their taxes she did not claim the money that she had received from Unemployment. Because he signed the tax return, assuming Marcy had filed honestly, Danny was stuck paying the back taxes along with the fines and penalties.

A VISIT TO THE ENCHANTED LAND

My husband and I were frantically trying to help Danny, but we didn't know what to do. We decided to ease the tension that the whole family was feeling, it might be a good idea to re-group, and take everyone to Disney World for a week. After all, who could be unhappy in Disney World, especially when all their expenses were being paid! Everyone seemed to enjoy the trip, even though Marcy would go out at night and leave Danny alone in their hotel room.

But when we got home from the trip my daughter and daughters-in-law told me that while they were in Disney World that Marcy told them that as soon as they got home she planned to divorce Danny. She knew that if she stayed with him for ten years she would be eligible for benefits from his company and alimony. That's when I exploded! I realized that she was "street smart" and we were only fooling ourselves that this marriage would ever work. The rest of our children, rightly so, thought she was *making a damn fool out of us. But they never interfered with the decisions their Dad and I made.*

We were fortunate that Danny's Boss called us one day and informed us that Marcy, without our knowledge, had changed Danny's Life Insurance Policy from his father and I to Marcy and her niece. We were thankful for his call and vowed to get this taken care of. They will never be able to pay back all the money we gave them, we're just thankful we have Danny home, and all expenditures must be approved by me.

THE DIVORCE

Marcy hired a divorce lawyer, which we had to pay for since her parents wanted nothing to do with her. In addition we gave her $4,000.00 cash so she could get out of Danny's life and get on with whatever she planned to do with the rest of her life. She did admit to me that she smoked crack cocaine at the mobile home, but she never implicated Danny.

THE GOOD SAMARITAN

Danny was still volunteering at the church bingo. One night a young girl, who probably knew that Danny was very vulnerable, asked if she could stay at his two bedroom mobile home for two weeks. She said she had just lost her son (she didn't say how, or the age of the child) and she needed a place to stay for just two weeks. About three weeks later she brought her boyfriend in to stay, he had just gotten out of prison. Soon they brought other men and women into Danny's home and he could not get them out, they wouldn't leave. He changed the locks on his door; they broke them and got in. They stole his television, VCR, tools, clothes, work boots and even his pet cat whom he loved.

My husband often would ride by Danny's mobile home in the evening, just to see if everything was quiet. One night he arrived there to see a swarm of police cars and people outside the home. Dad went up to one of the policemen to find out what was going on. The policeman told him it was none of his business and for him to leave immediately. He tried to tell the policeman that this was his son's home and that his son was head-injured and not able to get these people out of his home. The policeman either felt he could not or maybe did not want to hear this. He just insisted that Dad get away from the property immediately. Apparently the neighbors had been filing reports about suspected illegal activity at Danny's home. We were unable to find out who the police were investigating, or if any charges were ever filed against anyone staying at Danny's home. Thankfully, no charges were filed against Danny.

A week or so later we got a frantic call from Danny from a convenience store near his home, begging us to come over with $300.00 immediately as this man had a knife at his throat and was going to kill him. This hoodlum also had a big, fat woman with him. Danny had never known or associated with people like this in his life and he was scared to death of them. Mostly they were from Trenton and Philadelphia. And now we were also scared for they knew where we lived. My husband, fearing for Danny's life, took the money to them, but to be sure he didn't try to get away they slashed the tires on Danny's car. The next day the back window of our car was shot out as it was parked in our driveway.

TIME TO CALL IN THE LAW

Now we knew it was time to go to the police. We made an appointment and went to the police station to try to get some advice on how to handle this situation. The policeman came out with a stack of complaints that his neighbors had written. We were told to stay away from Danny's house because he was running a "crackhouse". I don't know if Danny knew this, but I suspected it, because he would bring his telephone bills here to be paid, and I have proof of all the calls that were made, sometimes 12 to 20 times a day, during the hours that Danny was at work, to places in Trenton and in and around Philadelphia. The police promised they would send one of their men to our house to sit and talk to us about this situation, but nobody from the police department ever came or even called us.

ON BEING VULNERABLE

Danny trusted everybody and especially if they let him think they were going to be his friend. One night one of these undesirables asked Danny to drive him to Princeton, NJ where he had to pick up some bicycles for his nephews who lived in Trenton. Danny drove him there and was sitting in his car waiting for his "friend" to come with the bikes, when a police car pulled up and arrested Danny for stealing bikes. Danny never suspected what this "friend" was up to, but nevertheless had to attend a hearing in NJ and make restitution in the amount of $400.00. Another night, Friday, his payday, some person or persons took him to Trenton, beat him up, stole his money, slashed his head open and left him in an alley to die. Somehow, we'll never know how, he was taken back here to Lower Bucks Hospital and left there to be stitched up. We never knew about this until a week later, when Danny asked his dad if he would take him to the hospital to have the stitches removed from his head. Ironically, they slashed him right along side where his shunt is placed.

LOSING IT ALL

Things were no better at work. He was bullied by his co-workers who thought they were being funny. Danny was their fall guy. For instance, one cold winter day when Danny had a bad cold they locked him out of the shop with no coat. It was snowing, and he had to walk around the back of the large building to get in a back door. Another time he came home from work with his shirt ripped straight down the front. When we asked him what he happened he said that one of the men at work, a professional boxer, got angry and ripped his shirt. They are only two of the incidents that we found out about. My husband and I should have taken action then with his bosses at work. But Danny didn't want us to do or say anything for fear he'd lose his job. All things considered, his job, his home life, people who he couldn't get to leave his home, no food and a dwindling bank account, it's no wonder Danny was angry all of the time. As soon as we saw his car pull up to our home, we knew he was going to rant and rave about the life he couldn't control.

Shortly after Danny's divorce we were called in to the office of his boss at the machine shop. He said that Danny had been a good and faithful worker for 21 years, but due to the events that transpired lately and his attendance, he was forced to lay him off (a nice way of saying he was being fired). We certainly didn't blame him, after all Danny worked on expensive machinery. He started coming in late for work or not coming in at all. This was not the Danny they knew. Was Danny on crack cocaine too? We'll never know. We couldn't recognize any of the symptoms, because we never dealt with a problem like this in our family.

Danny eventually lost his home and everything in it. The people who ran the mobile trailer park were very nice to us and very understanding. They asked me if there was anything in his home I wanted before they tore it down. I said the only thing I wanted was his baby book, which I started when he was born and kept till he got married. They had a security guard accompany me and I was able to salvage that important book.

BRINGING DANNY HOME

We took Danny home to live with us, which didn't sit well with our other children; I believe they were concerned about the safety of their dad and me. But we told them if one of them had suffered any kind of injury, we would never put them out on the street to fend for themselves. I think, after seven years, that issue has been resolved. But I must admit that we, too, were concerned when Danny moved back with us. We knew these people knew where we lived and might come here looking for money, or looking for Danny. His mobile home was torn down, so they couldn't go there. It took a long time for us (or at least me) to get over this fear.

SEEKING HELP

It was time for me to reach out for help in another direction. I started making phone calls, writing letters and contacting every agency I could find in the state, and almost always got the same answer: "we treat drug and alcohol problems, we don't have access to head injury problems". And the buck was passed again and again to yet another agency. Then I tackled the politicians, every representative, congressman, and senator, and even Governor Rendell. I got the same runaround, until I finally got a telephone call from the secretary of one of the politicians (God bless her!) who said she knew a lawyer in Philadelphia who had just handled a head injury case, and she was sure he would speak to us, which he did. My husband and Danny and I made three visits to his office (for which he didn't charge us!) and he took our case. He arranged a meeting with a social security judge with us in attendance, and the judge decided that Danny was indeed eligible for social security benefits. Some progress at last! We were told later by a person in our local social security office that Danny should have been eligible 21 years ago. We had contested the decision at the time, but they told us if Danny could wash dishes he was able to work. I honestly believe that since head injuries are invisible in most cases they are misdiagnosed. There are no wheel chairs, no walkers or canes, but you have to spend time talking to a head injured person to recognize the disability. Of course that was thirty-four years ago. Today, many hospitals have units for head injury. Danny now receives monthly social security benefits. His checks are sent direct deposit to his bank in my name for Danny since I am the only one who can withdraw money from his bank. Thus he is protected from unscrupulous people who would take advantage of him. And once a year I submit an accounting of the money he received to social security. We charge him a nominal amount for room and board, and he is responsible to pay for his clothes, gas, car maintenance & insurance, cigarettes, medical and dental bills, etc. After accounting for all of his bills, I give him some pocket money from his account for any small expenses he may have.

We had hoped, prayed, and worked for so many years that Danny would return to being an independent and productive member of society. What we have ultimately come to accept is that Danny is once again a child in our home, albeit an adult with a head injury, as opposed to a child. I am now 77 years old and in December my husband was 80. Our biggest fear is what will happen to Danny when we die. Our home will have to be sold and divided among our four children. Where will Danny live? Who will take on the responsibility for Danny's finances? We can't expect our other three children to take on Danny's responsibilities. Danny wouldn't know how to take over his bills and what it would cost him for an apartment, utilities, and groceries. When my husband and I are no longer here to manage Danny's SSDI payments, one of our other children will have to be assigned as his financial custodian.

About one year ago, while Danny was working the church Bingo, his ex-wife, Marcy, came to visit him. She is collecting either Social Security Disability or Welfare, we don't know which. But she told Danny that since they were both collecting benefits they should get together and rent a place and share the bills. This is what she is doing now with three or four other girls, and they don't get along with each other. Danny told her there was no way he would do that. First of all, he said, he's back living with his parents and he loves it. He has his own room, TV, air-conditioning, bathroom, and his Mom is in charge of all his money. He can't take a dime out of the bank unless I get it for him. That put an end to it!

He's also smart enough now to tell people who want to borrow money from him that he doesn't have any, his Mom handles it all. When he needs gas or cigarettes or anything else I get the money out of the bank for him.

When it is his time to go, Danny has a paid up funeral fund with a local funeral home. This fund is in his sister, Erin's name. She will have to manage his final arrangements. We had to set up the funeral fund so that one of Danny's brothers will inherit this responsibility if Erin should die first. We never would have dreamed of the possibility that one of our grandchildren may have to take responsibility for Danny in his later years. We are lucky to have a close-knit family who are willing to assume responsibility for him, but what happens to head-injured people who do not have people willing or able to care for them?

THE REALITY

How many TV shows have you ever watched where you've seen someone who has an accident and suffered a head injury, is in a coma for days or weeks or months and when they wake up all is well and the story picks up right where it left off—and they live happily ever after. Well let me tell you—that's not real life! The reality is that it takes a long, long time to accept that the child you raised, or the person you married is not the same person you knew before the accident that changed his/ her and your life. You'll mourn, you'll cry, you'll get angry, and then you'll get busy, real busy. Looking for doctors with many specialties, speech therapists, occupational therapists, hospitals and/or rehabilitation centers, dentists that know how to treat head injured individuals. For years I have searched book stores and libraries for information on head injury and how other families were coping with it. The most I came up with were books containing medical terms and advice, some good and some bad, but a lot of language that I, a lay person, could not understand. Therefore, I decided to write my own story about our family and what we've endured for the past thirty-four years.

MY LAST ENCOUNTER

My last encounter with "the system" occurred just recently. I say my "last" encounter because my spirit has been broken. I'm tired. I don't know what else to do. Last week Danny and I had a meeting with the O.V.R. (Office of Vocational Rehabilitation) counselor. We spent almost two hours with her, at the O.V.R. They said in a letter to us that they were removing Danny from their records. We never did find out why. As she asked Danny questions, he would look to me for answers. One question she asked him was "do you want to work and what kind of work do you want to do.?" So he pointed at me and said "She's the one that wants me to go to work.". I admitted that this has been a goal for at least 8 years; I want him to use the brain God gave him and not to be comfortable doing nothing for the rest of his life.

The counselor asked him what he does when he gets angry, he said "I just give the anger back.", I told him to tell her the truth—when he gets angry (and he only does this with me) he clenches both fists and punches his head as hard as he can. I used to tell him that he could block his shunt that way or burst it open—then he would be back in a coma. It didn't matter. So now I just walk out of the room and tell him he is not going to upset me with this behavior. Next he told the counselor "I'm stupid, I'm dumb, I have a brain injury, I can't do anything." The counselor looks straight at me and says "someone must have put those ideas in your head." I'm sure she was trying to implicate me, but she was dead wrong. I've done nothing but encourage him throughout these 33 years. This counselor has no idea how a head injured person thinks or communicates, and therefore isn't a very good judge of his abilities.

When I tried to explain to the counselor that my husband is 80 and I am 77 years old and our biggest concern is what would happen to Danny when we died. Her comment was, "Well, Estelle, you won't have to worry anymore when you're dead! You won't know what's going on here." My spiritual faith tells me that is not so. I expect when I die I will meet my parents, my 12 brothers and sisters and all the family and friends I love. Do her remarks sound professional to you? They don't to me !!!! Her cavalier comments did nothing to alleviate my concerns about Danny's future, and certainly did nothing to help us prepare for the possibility of him becoming self-sufficient.

Does anybody know anything about head injury that I don't? Who are they? Where are they? I feel I have lived with it for over 34 years and am no closer to understanding head-injury than I was on the day of Danny's accident. I have learned a great many things, but as a mother, it was my desire to "cure" him, rather than to learn to live with an adult child for the rest of my life.

It breaks my heart to see so many of our brave young men and women returning from these unjust wars with injuries, limbs missing, and in particular those with T.B.I. (Traumatic Brain Injuries). To say nothing about the ones who come home in coffins.

EPILOGUE

For thirty-four years I have met families who had a brain injured loved one, and didn't know where to turn. I visited book stores and libraries looking for information. All I found were medical terms that confused me more. I searched the internet. Just how many lay people can interpret medical terminology? I was looking for a book that told about the reality of having a head injured person in their life, and how they coped with their situations.

There were several other incidents that happened that I cannot include in this book, for they would be devastating if Danny would read them, and heaven forbid, remember them.

I hope that everyone who reads this book will be able to find the answers they need. I hope I've shed a little light on what can happen to a head-injured person, and to be on guard against the things we've endured. Unethical people can easily take advantage of your loved one. Be thankful for the good people who will step in and help you. Just keep in mind that every head injured victim is different, and often need to be treated differently. I am only telling you what we, as a family, endured for 34 years. And it never gets any easier. We still have issues that must be addressed.

And always remember, you think it can never happen to you, but—